D1482898

PAPER SCULPTURE

PAPER SCULPTURE
George Borchard

B T Batsford Limited

TT 870
- B 65
1973 b

© George Borchard 1973
First published 1973

ISBN 0 7134 2318 8

Filmset by Keyspools Limited, Golborne, Lancs
Printed by William Clowes Limited, Beccles, Suffolk
for the publishers B T Batsford Limited,
4 Fitzhardinge Street, London W1H OAH

Contents

Acknowledgment

I would like to thank Charles E Fraser for his
excellent photographs of my work, also Errol
Jackson who supplied the photographs for
figures 58 and 88; Herbert K Nolan for figures
84 and 85, and J Harvey for figures 68 and 90
and colour plate 5. I would thank, too, the
Museum Education Officer at Oxford City and
County Museum, Woodstock, for permission
to use Mr Harvey's photographs, and the
Museum Service of the Derbyshire Education
Committee, who originally commissioned
figure 89.

I am indebted to Docent Wieslaw Nowak,
Pro-rector of the Academy of Fine Arts in
Warsaw, who pointed out the importance of
the work of Professor W Jastrzębowski, and
drew my attention to the then newly-
published book *Wojciech Jastrezębowski (1884–
1963)* (Ossolineum 1971), which contains a rich
source of information. I myself had the good
fortune of being a pupil of Professor W
Jastrzębowski during the years 1936–39.

London 1973   GB

Introduction

On a journey we often subconsciously twist and curl a bus ticket or a piece of paper, to while away the time. Sometimes the 'creation' takes on a definite shape – a bird, a fish, a monster or some intriguing abstract form – and one becomes aware of paper's possibilities.

This book describes the specific ways in which paper can be used to make imaginative and attractive three-dimensional creations. The material is not expensive, and the few tools which are required can be found in most homes. There is no need for a special studio – a convenient working surface will do to start with.

Anyone between eight and eighty can learn how to create paper sculptures for their own enjoyment; they can also be a pleasing addition to the home; a highly original present; an inexpensive Christmas decoration; or used for display purposes.

Materials

A good quality paper which is smooth (but not shiny), pliable and springy is necessary: it can be tested by holding one corner of a sheet between the first two fingers and flicking the protruding tip with the thumb. Cartridge paper which is not too thick is good to begin with, but the type of paper depends on the size of sculpture that is intended. For smaller items a good quality writing paper can be used successfully. For larger sculptures a thicker drawing paper should be used, or some of the hand-made varieties – which are more expensive – are ideal to work with. The expression 'paper thin' is misleading, because many papers are quite heavy and, used imaginatively, can be fashioned into rigid and self-supporting sculptures.

It is important to buy paper in sheets, not rolls, and to keep the sheets flat, because it is extremely difficult to straighten tightly rolled paper. For larger creations thin card, which can also be bought in sheets, may be useful.

When making a coloured paper sculpture, use a matt surfaced paper which is coloured throughout, not merely surface coloured. Never paint paper sculptures. Moistened paper becomes limp and will not spring back into shape.

Tools

Scissors A long-bladed pair – not too heavy –
which should just balance in the hand to
enable one to work freely and make sweeping
cuts; a pair with shorter blades for cutting
smaller items, and for curling; and a pair
with short straight or curved blades for
more intricate work.

Knives One with a very sharp, short blade
(or a one-sided razor blade, if carefully
handled) for cutting; and a not very sharp,
easy to handle penknife, for scoring.

Rulers A wooden ruler with scale; and a
metal ruler to guide the knife along straight
lines.

A piece of thick cardboard for a working
surface – to ensure clean cuts on paper with
the sharp knife, and to protect the table top.
It should be renewed when too much cutting
has been done.

A set square or two for drawing parallel
lines (by sliding one set square along the
other, or along the ruler if only one set
square is available).

A compass

Pencil and rubber

Dowelling One or two pieces of varying
thicknesses.

An odd *knitting needle* or an *upholsterer's*
needle will be useful.

Pins, paper clips, stapler, gummed paper,
tape, *Sellotape* (*Scotch tape*) for fastening.

Adhesive – colourless, quick drying (*UHU*).

opposite
1   Tools

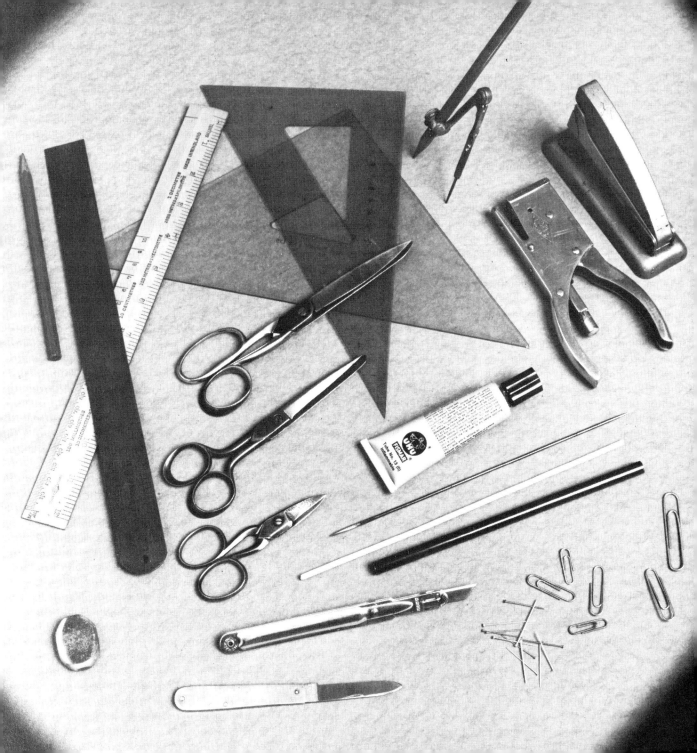

2 Contemporary 'Idyll': soft curved forms
juxtaposed with straight line protrusions

3 The two principal ways of shaping a flat
piece of paper into three-dimensional forms:
rolling; scoring and bending

One should be aware of a material's potentialities and limitations before starting to work with it. Paper bends easily, but only in one direction and always more or less geometrically (figure 2). It is important that the surface of the paper remains uncrumpled if the play of light and shadow is to be effective. Paper sculptures are composed of different planes, and the juxtaposition, alteration or even repetition of these shapes and planes creates harmony and rhythm.

Basically there are only two ways of making a three-dimensional formation from a flat piece of paper:
1 Rolling the paper
2 Scoring straight or curved lines with a knife, and then bending the paper along the scores.

Scoring is best done with a penknife which is not too sharp, thus scratching the surface but not cutting through the paper (figure 4). One should be particularly careful that all the edges are neatly cut, as jagged edges or torn pieces will spoil the most intricate piece of work.

Simple formations to investigate the possibilities of one piece of paper – by scoring and bending, cutting in and curling – are best to begin with. It will soon be discovered that paper can be made to represent anything but will not produce an imitation, like working in wax, clay or plaster will. Paper has a limited range of form but a virtually unlimited richness of expression: if it is treated gently and appropriately it will respond in astonishing and often unexpected ways.

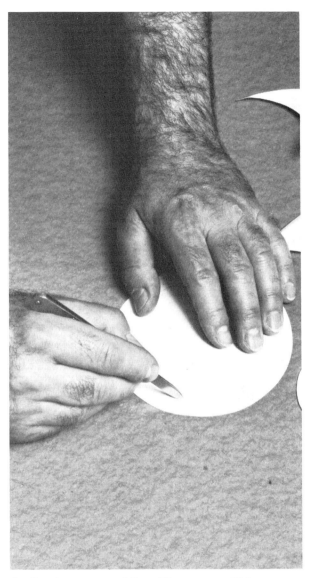

4 Scoring a curved line. The paper will be cut apart if the knife is too sharp

15

Simple creations from a rectangle

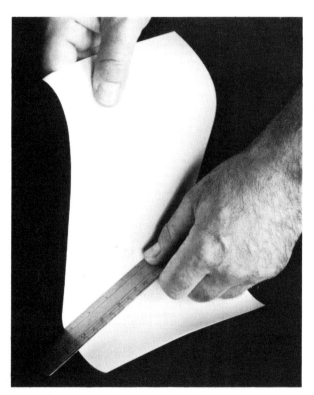

5   Curving a piece of paper using a wooden
ruler against the working surface

opposite
6   Tubes shaped from curved and rolled papers

Rolling

The simplest and most obvious way to transform a flat two-dimensional sheet of paper into a three-dimensional form is to roll it into a tube, ie a cylinder. Use paper clips at each end of the overlapping edges to keep it in shape, although the top edge will probably not stay in position because the sheet will be tending to pull back into its former flat shape.

To shape the cylinder more quickly and effectively, take a wooden ruler in one hand and place its edge on to a sheet of paper which you hold on to the working surface with the other hand. Press the ruler down gently and then pull the paper between the cardboard and the ruler. Immediately after the first treatment the sheet will start curving inwards, for the fibres of the paper are being pressed into a tubular form. Continue this treatment until the paper is curved sufficiently to enable the tube to stand freely on the table, without the aid of clips.

Give several sheets of paper this tube-forming treatment, along both the length and the width of the paper, and making loosely and tightly curved cylinders. Apply a quick drying adhesive to the outer, overlapping edges. Then combine the units into an interesting or complex arrangement (figure 6).

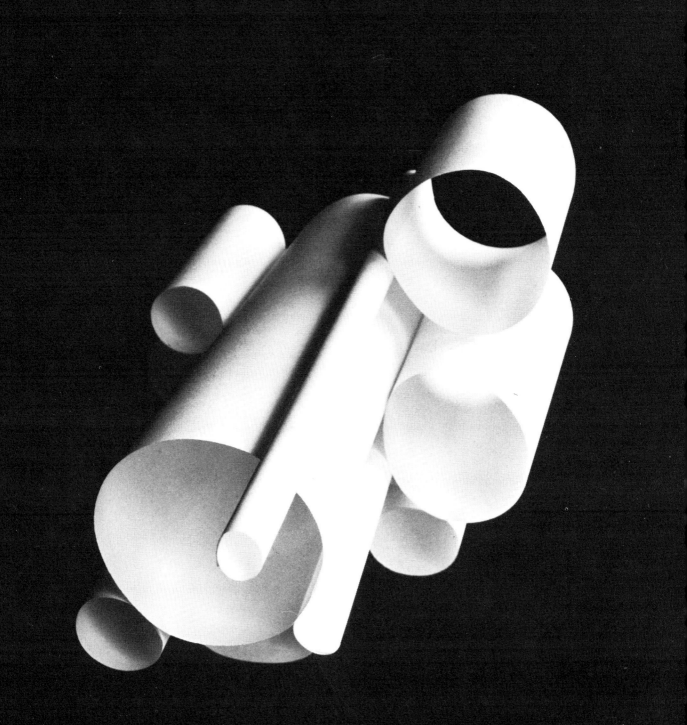

Scoring

Using a ruler, mark parallel lines at uneven intervals across the width of the paper. The lines can be marked with a pencil or, better still, with the tip of a penknife or the blade of a pair of scissors because this shows on both sides of the paper immediately.

Joint the marks by scoring along the lines with the penknife against the metal ruler, and give the paper the curving treatment described above. After several treatments bend the paper along the scored lines, firmly pressing along the ridges with the fingers: a slightly fluted formation takes shape.

Each section can be curved with the ruler; or the curves can be deepened by holding a ridge with the thumb and forefinger of each hand and pressing the next ridge forward with the middle fingers.

This kind of fluted formation is equally effective on either side (figure 7). It could be used to make a lampshade: instructions for this are given on pages 67 to 70.

Figure 8 shows four variations on this theme of using straight scored lines on one side of the sheet only. Scoring on both sides of the paper creates a concertina-type formation, and may be attempted next.

Mark unevenly spaced parallel lines on both sides of a sheet of paper; then score along the lines on both sides. Bend the paper along the scores which face you; then turn the paper over to bend the scores on that side.

There are endless variations on this theme, depending on the spacing of the lines, the different ways of pleating, and the way the pleating is handled (either held close together or pulled wide apart, seen vertically or horizontally, with the pleats squeezed together at one end, or in the middle with the free ends fanning out: figure 9).

8   Same-sized rectangular pieces, scored and bend on one surface only, formed into tubes

opposite
7   Fluted formations are equally effective on either side

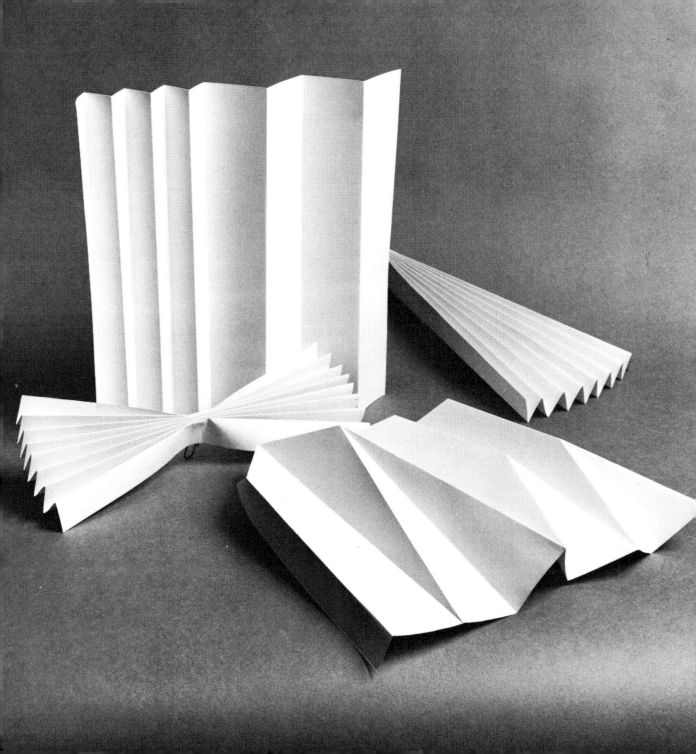

The crispness of the pleating depends on scoring neatly along the metal ruler, and making the lines really straight. After trying several kinds of pleating, it may be interesting to attempt a variation, such as the one shown in the foreground of figure 9.

Take a piece of paper with fairly wide pleating. Spread it out on the cardboard working surface and start marking, as shown in figure 10:

1 Mark off distance AB on the ridges facing you
2 Score lines from B to C
3 Bend paper along scores BC
4 This necessitates reversing creases AB

The reversed formation has an interesting, sculptural appearance, and variations on this theme are possible, depending upon the angle of the 'V' line (B to C) and its placing along the ridges. (See also figure 72).

A further use of straight scored lines may be to mark diagonal lines across the sheet, first one way and then the other. Bend the paper along these scores and an interesting surface results (figure 11). Another variation is to score wavy lines across a sheet of paper and gently bend along these: this gives a rather surprising effect. Start off with simple lines and let the imagination run riot (figure 12).

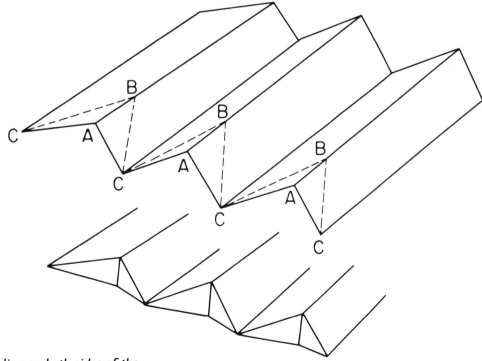

opposite
9 Scoring and bending on both sides of the paper forms concertina type pleating

10 How to reverse pleating

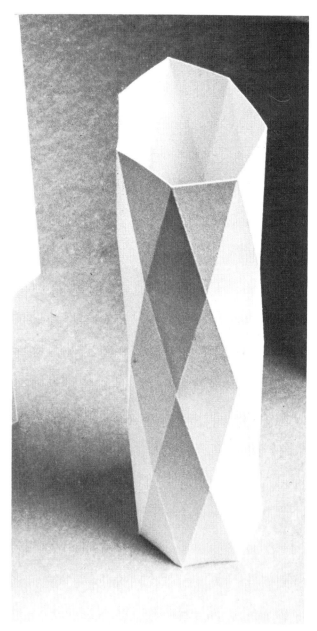

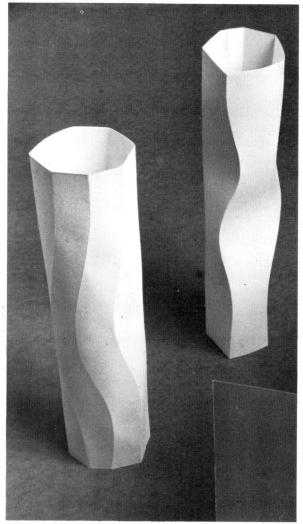

12   Curved lines scored and bent on one side
of the paper

left
11   Scoring and bending diagonally on one side
of the paper

Discs

Discs are good, basic shapes which can be used in many ways in paper sculpture. With a compass draw a number of equal circles on a sheet of paper. Cut them out carefully so as to retain their clear curved outlines, and then shape them into three-dimensional forms by scoring the surfaces in different ways, and bending the paper along the scored lines as shown in figure 13. Cone formations are easily made from discs: cut a straight line from the circumference of the disc to the centre (ie along the radius). Start shaping the cone by sliding one edge over the other: the greater the overlap, the steeper the cone will become and the more the base will shrink.

In figure 14 the disc in the right hand corner has been formed into a flat cone. The two cones next to it were made from half discs of the same size as the cut out in which they are standing. The more complex formations are made by drawing varying numbers of circles within each disc and then scoring along these lines. Remember that when you score along one line the paper will bend away from you – so the next circle should be drawn and scored on the other side of the paper.

To bend along the scores, hold the paper between the thumb and first finger, push the ridge under with the second finger of one hand and bend the formation into shape with

13 Discs of equal size scored and bent in different ways

23

the fingers of the other hand (figures 15, 16). This is the way to shape any formation with curved lines.

It is important to remember that any form created from a flat shape will cover a smaller area than the shape itself, because the paper is drawn upwards into the third dimension. This has to be taken into consideration when making a specifically sized sculpture.

opposite
14   Cone formations, using discs of equal size. Simple cones are shaped by overlapping; complex ones by scoring lines as required, bending the paper and overlapping along the cut from the edge of the disc to the centre

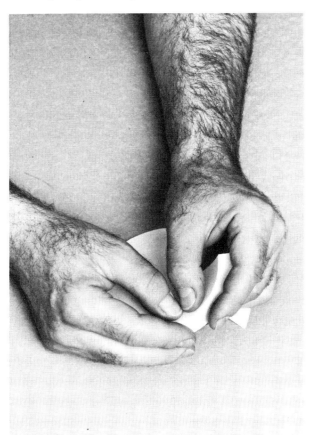

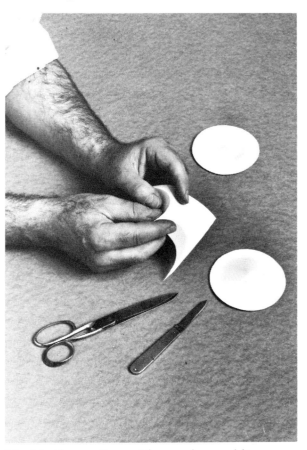

15   How to bend the paper along scored curved lines

16   Shaping an item with scored curved lines

Further developments

So far paper has been used to make various simple but attractive creations. It is now time to experiment further: start with concertina pleating, which is an easy formation.

Take a piece of paper and pleat it concertina fashion at irregular intervals, in pairs. Then press any one fold firmly at the ridge where the two layers meet. Next make two parallel cuts, either at right angles to the ridge, or any other way, down to the next ridge where the paper folds. Open the pleating and push through the part which lies between the two cuts to obtain an interesting spatial, architectural form. Make several similar cuts, draw the folds closer together or further apart, and observe the light and shadow effects. Continue to experiment in this way, but remember two cuts are always necessary. They can be parallel or at angles to each other (figure 17), but if it is simple pleating be careful not to make cuts in one fold, and at the same level in the adjoining pleating, or a strip may be cut off completely.

If the pleats are fairly deep, and this kind of protrusion is to be repeated in adjacent pleats at the same level, it is better to make cuts half-way into the pleats. Then lift the bit lying between the cuts, with the knitting needle, to reverse the pleating, and press gently at the base (see the lampshade on the standing lamp in figure 72). Making the cuts at an angle to the ridges gives fascinating and sometimes unexpected results (figure 18).

opposite
17 Complex surface treatment of concertina type pleating: cutting into the folds and reversing the pleats at right angles

18   Cuts into concertina formations can be
varied by using differing angles and numbers
of cuts

Stars

Stars can be made from square sheets of paper.

To make a perfect square from a sheet of paper

1 Measure off a square with a ruler *or*
2 Lift the bottom corner of the sheet up, so that the side edge neatly covers the upper edge. Make a crease along the diagonal, and cut off the single strip of paper that is left. This gives a perfect square.

To make a star

Take a square piece of paper which has a diagonal fold down it, as above. Fold along the other diagonal as well. Open up the square and turn it over onto the other side. Fold it in half one way, and then the other, making sure that all the lines cross in the centre (figure 19). Then press firmly along the creases of the middle lines, pushing the centre outwards and pressing the diagonal folds firmly until a star shape forms.

   Make a few more stars, varying the pressure on the folds to give a variety of shapes (figure 20). So far only creasing has been mentioned, not scoring, since the former gives a sturdier construction. It is easy to do and will help stars retain their shape

19   Folding a square to make a star

20   Stars made from same sized pieces of paper

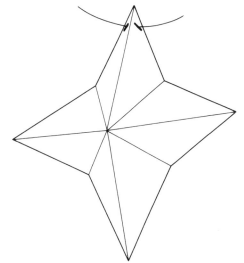

21 Making a cut so the star can hang on a thread

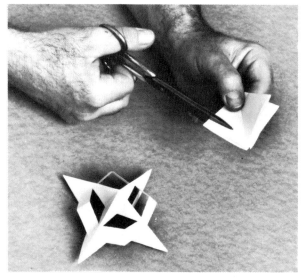

22 To make the stars more varied two cuts are made from the middle creases towards the diagonals

better. Scoring, however, is advisable if stout cartridge paper is used.

Display

Stars look most effective strung on a thread and hung across the room. Either use a threaded needle, piercing through the two layers of paper near one of the tips; or make an oblique cut upwards, from the edge near the tip. The star can then be hooked onto a thread which has been strung across the room (figure 21). The whiteness of the paper sparkles attractively, particularly in candlelight.

Developments

This kind of star can be made much more intricate and varied. Make several simple stars on which to experiment. After folding the paper along the diagonals and into half each way, hold the centre where all the creases meet between the fingers, as shown in figure 22. Then make two parallel cuts from the middle creases towards the diagonal lines, but do not cut as far as the lines themselves! Then place one of the sections with the cuts against the two remaining sections and make the same cuts in these. Open the star and push the centre outwards. Then, with the tip of the scissors or a knitting needle, gently lift the strips between one set of cuts and reverse the fold. Press at the base of the strip so it will stand away from the surrounding surfaces. Repeat this treatment with the remaining three strips, and a new star formation is the result (figures 22, 23).

It is possible to make a variety of patterned stars using this method. Remember that two cuts are always necessary for one strip to appear. Try cutting in on the diagonals (the long creases between the tips of the stars); the strips must be pushed inwards, not outwards, with this pattern, and the results are not as effective as when cuts are made on the shorter middle creases (figures 25–8). The cuts need not be straight, nor pulled parallel. The only important point is that the cuts should never go from one crease to the next crease, or the star will disintegrate: but perhaps it is better to learn by making the mistake.

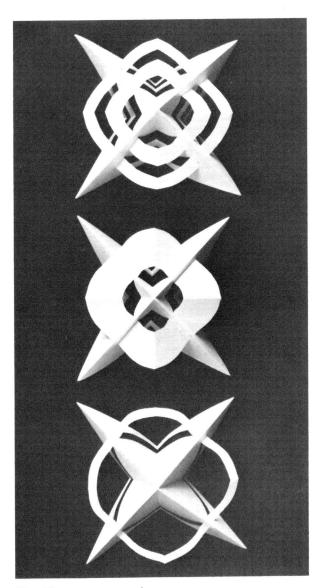

23   *Variations on a theme*

24   *The cutting is now done along the diagonals towards the middle creases, and the bits are reversed to the back*

25

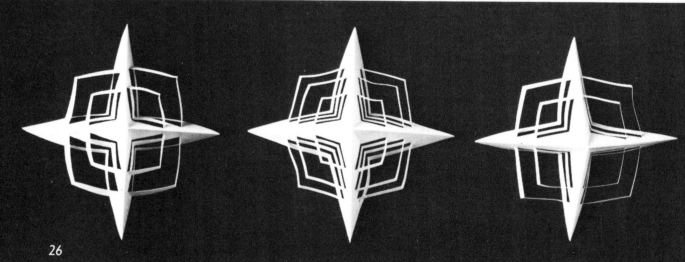

26

25–28 *Variations in cutting and shaping the stars*

opposite Plate I *Detail of* St George and the Dragon *see also figure 88*

27

28

33

29 *Stars made from discs*

To make a star from a disc

Stars can also be made from paper discs, folded along the diameters. First fold the paper disc in half, unfold it, and then fold along the other diameter by matching the ends of the first one and creasing the paper. The disc is thus divided into quarters, with all the folds on the same side of the disc. Now halve the quarters by matching one end of a diameter over the next diameter, pressing firmly along the crease, and repeating the procedure until the paper has been divided into eighths. Turn the disc over and halve the segments in the same way, until it has been divided into sixteenths.

The paper should not be too thick – a good writing paper would be pleasant to handle and would give crisp creases. Firmly press the folds on one side and then on the other, until a star-like formation appears, like the one in the near corner of figure 29. As was mentioned before, the more the creases are drawn together, the steeper the formation and the more the base will shrink; this must be borne in mind if the intention is to make something of a specific size.

These stars can be cut and shaped in the same ways that the four pointed stars and the concertina folding were decorated – and there are endless variations of this theme (figure 30).

opposite
30 *Endless possibilities on a theme*

Crocodragons

These crocodragons (figure 31) look intriguing but they are quite easy to make, despite their complex-looking body shapes, provided the previous exercises have been completed and paper has been handled in the different ways described.

The bodies are based on simple concertina folding, the only difference being that the paper is not a rectangular piece, but a strip which tapers towards one end (the tail). The divisions are wide apart at the broader end of the paper, but get nearer together towards the tail. The three-dimensional effect is obtained by scoring 'V' lines along the edges and reversing the pleating (see figures 9 and 10). The bumpy shapes along the centre of the back are made by cutting into the protruding pleats and reversing the creases inwards.

The heads are made from square pieces of paper which have been scored and shaped into curves along one side, between two corners. The opposite corners are overlapped on the underside, forming the cone-shaped snouts. The eyes are rolled pieces of paper which are stuck in position to give the beast an expression. (Placing the eyes differently creates a whole range of looks).

(The dragon's head in figure 88, *St George and the Dragon*, was created in a similar way. The dragon's body consists of a number of sheets cut in zigzag line from one long edge of a sheet towards the opposite one – but leaving the parts to hang together. The loose ends are then stapled over each other, making the paper curve. Finally the ends of the zigzags are curled upwards, and the different sections pieced together by fixing them to the background).

opposite
31 Amusing 'Crocodragons'; the bodies are made from complex concertina pleating, the cone-shaped heads are formed by scoring

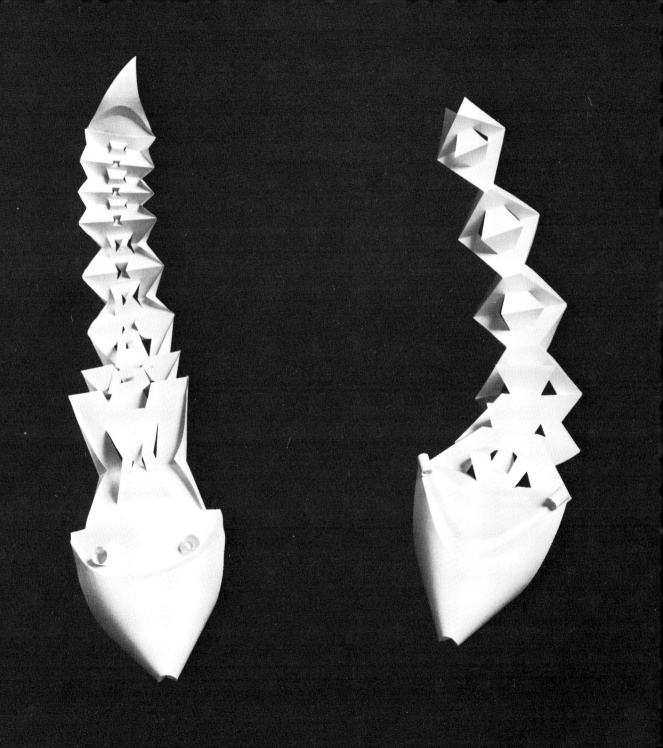

Faces

So far simple, basic paper sculpture forms have been developed to see how they turn out. Experiments with the first form – the tube – will also produce some interesting results. Make several short tubes which, with a few simple additions, can be transformed into 'faces', as seen in figure 32 a, b, c, d. Paper imposes limitations so our ideas about the human face, its character and expression, must be simplified.

Eyes are very important parts of the face. Start by piercing two holes in the tube and then make them round by twisting the scissors. Make a jab with the scissors where the mouth should be.

To make the eyes more expressive place short rolled pieces of paper into the holes; squeeze these slightly and the tension of the unwinding paper will keep them in position. It is great fun to make the eyes look in different directions, or even to make them peer by lengthening or shortening the coils.

Another way of indicating eyes is by cutting two short curves into the surface of the tube, and then curving the 'lids' upwards. Do not cut them out, as this would create a hole, which is two-dimensional: the eyelid is a sculptural form. Another variation of eye shaping is to cut out pairs of half moons, curve them, and try them with the curved edges against the face. Again slight variations, not only in placing but in the curves creates a whole range of expressions. Placing eyes in relation to each other on a number of tubes makes an interesting object lesson in how to create different types of facial expression.

Nose It may not be necessary to indicate a nose on the simplified paper sculpture 'face'. On the other hand some types of face need a slight indication or even a very pronounced nose. A crease of the paper, as in figure 32 c and d may be sufficient. To soften the top edge of the nose, the paper can be cut into strips and curled inwards or outwards, which is an excellent opportunity to try out some elementary hair styles.

Mouth This can be indicated, as was mentioned previously, by a simple straight or curved cut with the scissors, and a slight pressing in of the paper at the top edge to heighten the expression. Alternatively, a slot can be made into which a folded strip is inserted, with its ends rounded and curved, the top up and the lower down. Choosing the right length of lips for a particular face is interesting and amusing, see figures 32 d and 58.

opposite
32 a b c d   Tubes made into faces

Character

A complex face with more 'character' can be made as follows. Make a tube. Take a wide strip of paper and cut two 'U' shapes each side of a narrow strip – which will be the nose – as in figure 33. A fringe is cut along the other long edge of the wide strip as well as into the parts adjacent to the 'U' cut outs. The fringe can be curled with the help of scissors, using an upward movement along the strips, which are placed between the closed scissors and the thumb. A hair-do helps to define the character.

The formation is fixed to the 'face' in such a way that the nose part stands away slightly from the curve of the tube. The fixing is done at the back of the head. The two inverted 'U' cut-outs appear to be the eyebrows, casting a shadow on to the part where the eyes are placed, thus achieving a more sculptural appearance. The nose can be shaped according to fancy – curled inwards (or even outwards is effective) – as long as the play of light and shadow is taken into consideration.

Chin The two characters in figure 33 are quite dumpy: a slimmer-looking face can be made by choosing different features, perhaps a slimmer chin, which can be done very easily. A more pronounced chin is made by cutting a curve into the lower part of the tube, a jaw line from ear to ear. Part of the neck can be curved inwards, or rolled into a tube to make the chin stand out (figure 34).

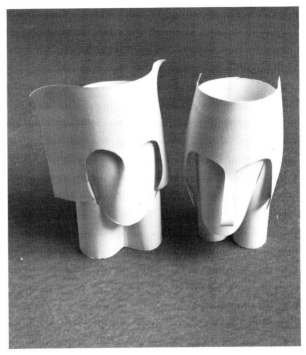

34 Shaping the chin – made by cutting into the tube – creates a more vivid character

opposite
33 Variations on a theme: the same shaped nose and hairpiece applied in two different ways makes a great difference

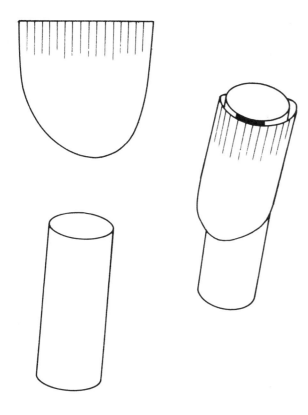

35 Making a more interesting character by using separate parts for the neck and face to enable any angle or tilt of the head

opposite
36 At the races (1905)

Another method would be to make a tube for the neck first, and then a separate piece for the face, made from a rectangular piece of paper with a curved line cut at one end, and the top left straight (figure 35). Cut the curve generously: it can always be cut down to suit the character. The straight piece of the 'face' can be finely fringed to form part of the hair-do. The face part is fixed to the neck at the top edge with a piece of *Sellotape* (*Scotch tape*), to allow for flexibility when adjusting the curved sides to the back of the neck. 'Making faces' in paper sculpture is great fun: expressions can be created by varying the placing and shaping of the nose pieces, hair-styles and eyebrows.

Faces and figures

Figure 2 is a composition showing the different ways of using paper sculpturally. The curves shaping the two people contrast well with the straight, upright lines of the buildings, with their angular features highlighting the character of contemporary architecture.

In figure 36 contrasts again create interest: protruding parts are shown off by less curving surfaces, cut and curled strips contrast with plain forms, and texture is added by cuts with a sharp knife, the pattern curving upwards to stand out. The hat decorations are made by cutting, in a continuous spiral line, into a rectangular piece of paper, and curling it in sections, one way and the other.

In figure 37 the dress of the ballad singer in the Art Nouveau frame has been formed by scoring simple lines, and bending the paper. The sleeves were made by overlapping surfaces (as when shaping cones). The idea is to use the paper in a way that will give an effective contrast between light and shadow.

The Regency frame (figure 38) looks intricate, but with the exception of the curly beading, one is now capable of making it – and in no time the curving part will be mastered as well.

Take a long strip of paper. Hold one end firmly with one hand and pull the length across a wooden ruler pressed against the thumb of the other hand. Press gently otherwise part of the strip may tear. The paper starts to curl after the first treatment (figure 39). Repeat the treatment and the resulting spiral will be quite a surprise.

For the Regency frame a beading which curls regularly is required. This can be achieved by firmly winding the curled strip round a knitting needle or a piece of dowling as shown in figure 40. The spiral twist can be adjusted to make it even when placing it in position and fixing it with glue. The curling process can successfully be performed with the bland edge of some long scissors pressed against the thumb: this is more convenient when forming small, intricate pieces, as was mentioned when tackling hairstyles for faces.

The foilage of the tree in figure 38 is made by cutting a zigzag spiral-wise line into a

37 Ballad singer (1895)

38 Out in the park (1800)

rectangular piece of paper. Afterwards the tips are curled and the outside end fixed under the formation.

In figure 41 the lady's dress and sleeves are formed by scoring on one side only, creating the gently curving surface. The Neo-Gothic decorations are cut out and a line scored following the pattern of the design. Then the paper is bent along the score.

'Pop Singer' (figure 42) effectively contrasts the gently curving surfaces of the paper with the deep pleating. The dimple in the sleeve of the bent arm is an inverted cone, the centre of which is at the end of a cut in the straight sleeve, to enable bending.

Encounter 1875 (figure 43) uses techniques which have already been discussed. Paper sculpture lends itself admirably to such historical costumes and three-dimensional fashion plates, and gives plenty of scope for imaginative handling.

overleaf
41   Little friend (1830)   Simple scoring creates the dress, curled strips help to build up the coiffure

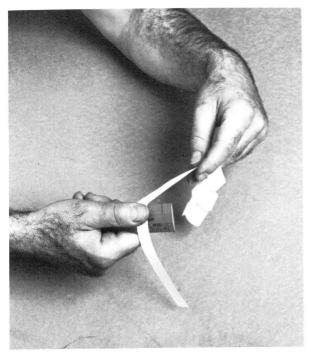

39   Curling a strip of paper by passing it gently between the ruler pressed against the thumb

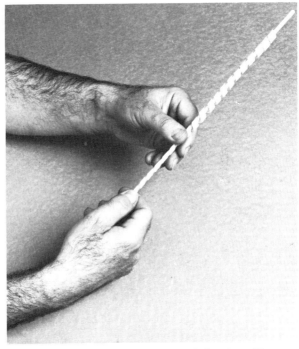

40   Wind the curled strip round the dowelling and press gently to make a spiral. This has been used for the 'period' frame in figure 38

42　Pop singer　*Gently curving parts are set off by the deep folds of the pleating*

43　Encounter (1875)　*Contrasts of light and shadow on the more elaborate parts are set off by the gently curving surfaces*

Creations in the round

So far the emphasis has been on paper sculpture creations which are made to be seen against a background, allowing a frontal view only, apart from the preliminary formations which could be seen front and back. The next step is to create sculptures which are meant to be seen from every angle.

An important consideration with this type is that any join in the paper should either be part of the design (and therefore emphasised) or discreetly hidden. Any formation in the round can be self-supporting as long as careful consideration is given to the type and sturdiness of the paper, and the creation is not too asymmetrical or large (otherwise a support, hidden of course, will be necessary).

Start with the simple but effective formations shown in figures 45–48. These look rather complex but are easy to make. Take several rectangular pieces of paper. Fold the first piece in half, either along the width or the length. Then measure margins parallel to the two edges, opposite the fold, and score along these lines, on the outsides, keeping the paper folded. Cut at regular intervals from the fold down to the scored line (actually lines, as the paper is kept folded) at right angles. When cutting hold the folded paper between thumb and first finger, using the tips of the second and third fingers as a support for the scissors, which are held in the other hand. After making a cut keep the scissors in position and move *the paper* forwards.

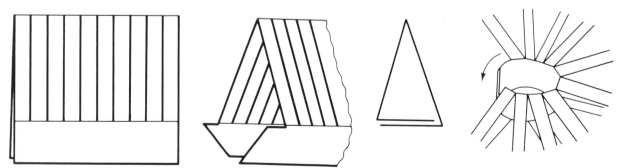

44   *Ways of making rosette formations*

When the cutting has been done, bend the margins away from the newly cut strips (this is quite easy, with the scored lines). Cut away the first pair of strips from the margin. Give the margins the curling treatment with the closed scissors, place one margin over the other and bend them into a circle, gluing the small bit where the strips have been cut away, under the other end. This gives the intriguing-looking formation shown in figure 45.

Figure 46 seems more complicated, but this is not the case. Only additional scored lines, parallel to the margins, are needed, one

opposite
Plate 2 Details from large 'Edwardian' sculpture in preparation. Face made from one piece of paper by scoring and bending

each side of the paper and somewhere nearer to the fold. Having done this, proceed in the same way as with the first formation and bend the strips along the scored lines.

Figure 47 is exactly the same as figure 46 with one variation: when bending along the scored lines, reverse the middle fold, and bend it inwards. It makes a great difference!

Figure 48 is one of the many variations which are possible on this same theme, and which can be explored to the heart's delight. Instead of cutting the strips at right angles to the fold, cut at another angle (but the strips must be parallel). Bend the strips along a scored line parallel to the ridge, each side of the folded paper, as with the previous formations. The strips should be fairly narrow, otherwise the cylinder formed by the rolled margins will have an angular appearance.

45   Simple rosettes with strips cut at right angles to the ridge

46   Rosette with scorings along the strips, on both sides of the ridge

There is nothing wrong with this, provided one likes it that way.

One thing should always be kept in mind: the scoring should only scratch the surface. If the knife is too sharp it cuts through the paper, and when it is bent it just falls apart. It was suggested at the beginning of this exercise that several pieces of paper of equal size should be prepared. If the pieces have been folded one way at the beginning, try folding them in the other for different results.

Another variation – instead of overlapping one margin over the other, place the left corner of the top margin over the right corner of the bottom one, so the margins continue in a spiral. To get an even better spiral effect try bending the margin outwards on another piece. Continue sliding one margin over the other, and soon something

unexpected will result (figure 49 b).

Figure 49 has not been folded lengthwise like the other; instead parallel cuts were made between the two scored margins. Then the strips were curved with the ruler against the working surface. Afterwards the spiral shaping was done to give a shell-like effect. Again there is a wide range of possibilities – not only varying the width of the paper, but cutting the strips differently as well. When cutting the strips with the sharp knife against the metal ruler, do it on the cardboard to get really clean cuts, which enhance a well-made paper sculpture.

opposite
49 a b Intriguing shell-like formations following on from the rosettes

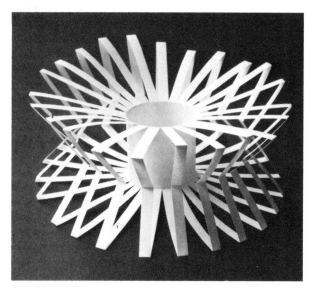

47   Rosette with scorings along the strips and reversed pleating along the ridge

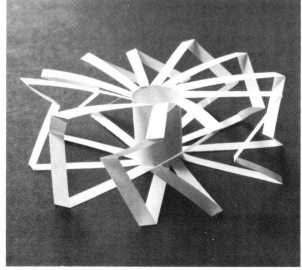

48   Strips for this rosette were cut at an angle to the ridge, lines were scored each side of the ridge, and the folding on this was reversed

50

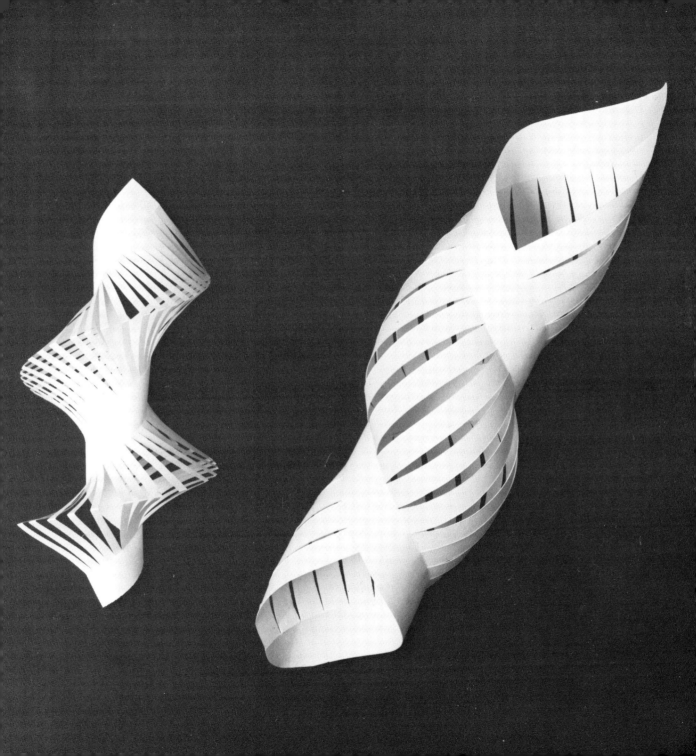

Tree formations

The tree formation shown in figure 50 combines ways of using and manipulating paper which have been discussed previously, to obtain three-dimensional effects. The tree trunk and base are two different forms of the cone. The foilage part is similar to the flower-star shown in figures 45–8.

Method

Follow figure 51: take a rectangular piece of paper, folding edge AB to cover AB1. Crease along AC – which is the diagonal of the square – and cut off at B1C. Open the paper out.

Now fold AB1 to match AB2 at diagonal AC. Press crease AD and cut off at AB2D. Take a compass and, with the point at A draw the sector from B to the diagonal, as shown in figure 51. Cut along this curved line and shape the paper into a cone, using a ruler to curl it. Glue the overlapping edges.

Cut off triangle B2DC and draw the largest possible circle in it. Cut out the circle, and make a cut to the centre, along the radius, so as to shape it into a shallow cone.

Piece ADB2 is a double layer of paper, folded along AD. Score a margin each side of the folded paper, along AE. Next cut equal strips, parallel to DE, starting from

50 Tree made from two cones – trunk and base – and foliage similar to the shell formations

crease AD up to the marginal scored line AE. At first it may be necessary to mark the divisions along the fold, to be able to cut regularly, but with confidence the cutting can be done by judging the distances. Cut as far as possible up to the top.

Bend the margins away from the strips, so one margin will tend to overlap the other. Give them the curling treatment, letting them pass between thumb and the bland edge of the scissors. Glue one over the other.

Fix the thin end of the 'foliage' to the top of the steep cone (the 'trunk') and, when the glue has dried – a quick drying adhesive is best – start winding the strip formation with the margins round the stem. It will soon be clear whether to wind tightly or leave a gap between the spirals: once this is decided fix the wide end in position along the trunk.

Finally, put some glue along the bottom inside rim of the trunk and gently press this on to the shallow cone, making sure that the joins on trunk and base match (this will be turned away from view). The tree will now be free standing, like the one in figure 52.

Now make another tree, but cut the strips differently. Cut them at right angles to the fold, which will of course start slightly higher above D, with the first cut finishing at E, and the others parallel to this one, leading up to the margin. The finished tree will very much resemble the one in figure 50. Slight variation in the angle of the strips can be explored in further experiments.

So far one square of paper has been used to make one tree. Try using two different sized squares – one for the trunk, and the other for the spiral foliage part.

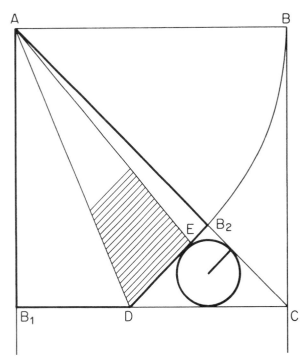

51　Making a tree

Another variation would be not to fold the part intended for the foliage: proceed in the following way (figure 53). Fold AB to AB1, firmly press along crease AC, and cut along AC and B1C. Of these two triangles one will be the trunk (by drawing the sector B to B2), and the other will be used for foliage. Measure AB1 to AB2, at this point draw a line at right angles (with set square) to join B1C in D. AB1C is a right angle. Cut along DB2. Now score two margins, starting from A along each side line as indicated in figure 53. Mark off equal distances along those margins and cut with a sharp knife along the metal ruler, following the lines up to the scores. Then bend the margins gently away from the strips, turn the paper over and apply the curling treatment across the strips with the ruler. Fix one margin over the other and continue making the tree, as usual. This sort can be seen in the forest in figure 54, third from the right.

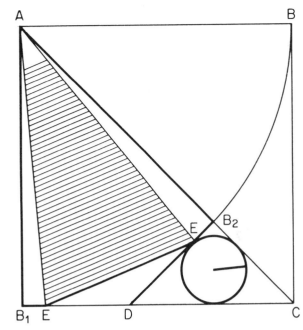

53   Making curly foliage with no ridges

opposite
52   Variation: the strips were cut at an angle
to the ridge

54   *A forest*

55 *Making a standing figure with a bottle as a support*

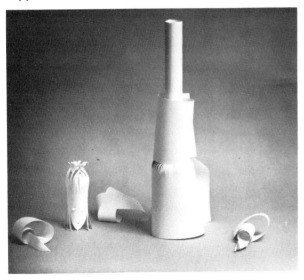

56 *The standing figure is shaped as the parts are assembled*

Medium-sized free standing creations in the round, based on a large cone or pleated formation, can effectively form part of a long garment on a figure. This will work well as long as the top part is not so asymmetrical and flamboyant that the figure topples over. The work could be steadied by assembling it on a bottle half filled with water or sand, as long as the figure is in a long garment. Start with simple formations, paying attention to the play of light and shadow (figures 55–7).

The display of schoolboys' heads with their various caps in fact hides unpleasant looking plastic dummies. Heads like these can be made over empty paint tins, with some sand to weight them down. Over the tin goes a tube rolled from coloured paper which forms the basis of the face, and is fixed to the neck, at the back. There is ample paper for the face part at the top, so it can be cut into strips which are curved and by overlapping form the roundness of the head. This allows the cap to rest on the head in a more natural way. To make the eyes rather vivid, cut the whites from gummed labels and stick them on. The coloured part of the eye is a rolled piece of paper inserted into an aperture which is pierced with scissors and then twisted round (or one may use a pencil to do this).

overleaf
57 *The lady has emerged – the supporting bottle is invisible*

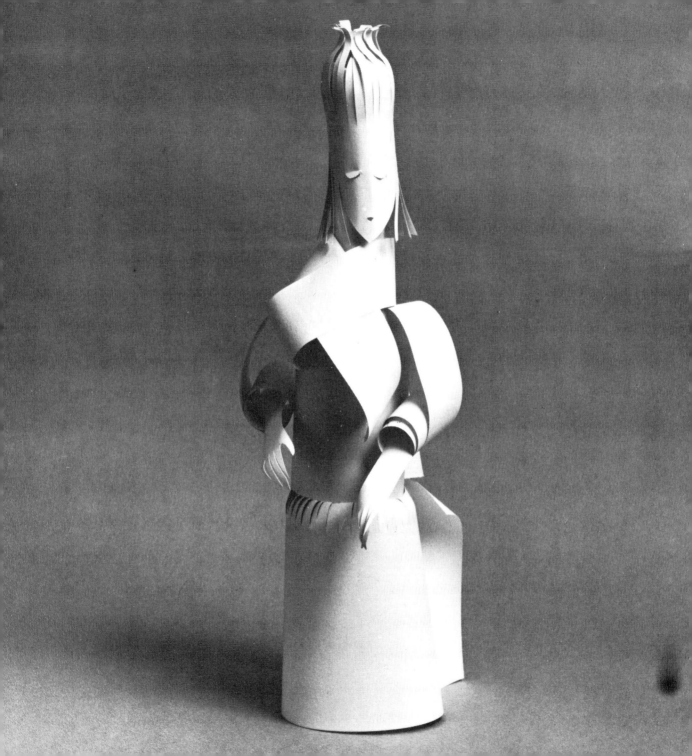

58   *Display of old cricket caps,* Childhood
Exhibition, *Camden Arts Centre, London 1967*

Larger paper sculptures

As mentioned previously when designing a paper sculpture in the round, which will not be self-supporting, some sort of invisible construction inside is necessary. This need not be elaborate. A firm base made from a medium-sized plywood disc and dowelling fixed into drilled holes in strategic places will do the trick. Cross sections of pieces of battens will prevent any parts of the formation sagging or even collapsing. This sort of preparation is invaluable if the work is to proceed without hitches.

What to make: preparations

If the material is treated in a sympathetic way, it will help you to sense what thickness of paper would be appropriate for a specific piece of work. It is desirable to improvise with the details, but it is important to know right from the start what is intended, and what size it will be. Once the idea has formed, make a full scale sketch. A few lines with a piece of charcoal or chalk will give an idea of the size of the finished work, the various parts and their relation to each other. The gist of the creation must be there on the paper. Large sheets of wrapping paper can be used for the sketch, if necessary several fixed together. The sketch will give an indication of what sort of support the paper sculpture will require, and at what angle it should be constructed. But remember that the sketch is two-dimensional, and the creation will be in the round, so it is important to start thinking in those terms.

Another point must be stressed right now: where will the finished work be seen? If it is to be moved elsewhere, now is the time to decide how it is going to be moved or if it would be better to make it in pieces and assemble it at its destination. From this point of view the sketch is invaluable. The question of packing can cause headaches so take the following advice: if the sketch shows a fair-sized creation, try to get hold of a couple of discarded cartons and make a special container – strong and suitable for its particular purpose – for when the paper sculpture is ready.

Sculptures

The double-faced dancer (figures 59–67) did start, as can be seen, as a rough sketch of an idea (but a cardboard box of the right size was at hand, for transporting it).

The figure of the dancer is made from simple forms based on the cone and the tube. Each arm is made from one long rectangular piece, put in at right angles where the elbows bend. At the end of these cuts a small circle is drawn, where an inverted cone can soften the angularity of the elbow. Bend each section of the arms into tubes and glue the overlapping edges. Before bending the arms it is necessary to cut out a bit at the forearm, to enable the elbow to bend. The grimacing mask is made from one rectangular piece with the addition of the mouth.

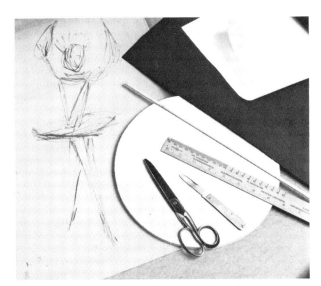

59   Preparations for a free standing figure of a dancer – sketch (essential), base, dowelling and papers

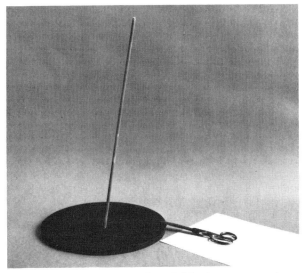

60   The base is covered with black paper, and an appropriate length of supporting dowelling is fixed at the requisite angle

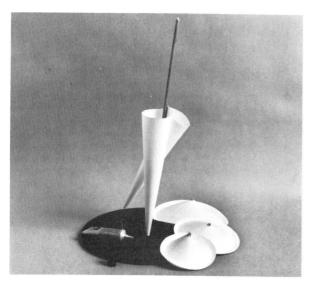

61 Dancer's legs and parts of the costume are prepared and gradually fixed in position

62 Layers of the ballet skirt are glued to the support

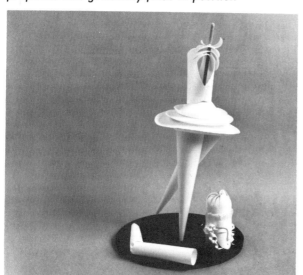

63 The bodice and neck frill are ready for the head to be placed in position

64 The arms, with sleeve decorations, are fixed and opposite 65 The dancer emerges . . .

It is great fun to use only one piece for the main formation, scoring, cutting in and bending the sheet, with unexpected – perhaps even unsatisfactory – results. Figure 67 shows a simplified diagram of the dancer's mask. Try a few variations: altering the parts, varying the degree of overlap, creating a three-dimensional effect, and getting the right expression, according to fancy.

66   *and turns round to show a different expression*

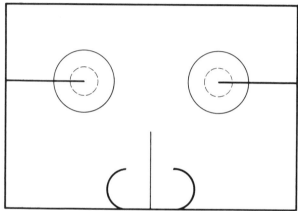

67   *The dancer's mask*

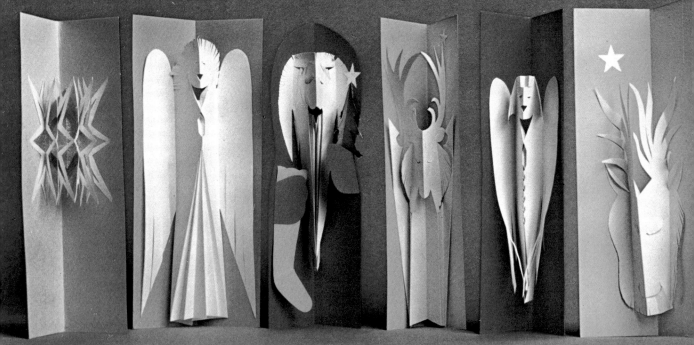

opposite
Plate 3   Christmas crib
Plate 4   Christmas cards

68 a b   Lady of 1875   This creation in the round is supported by two sticks, one of which continues up to the head

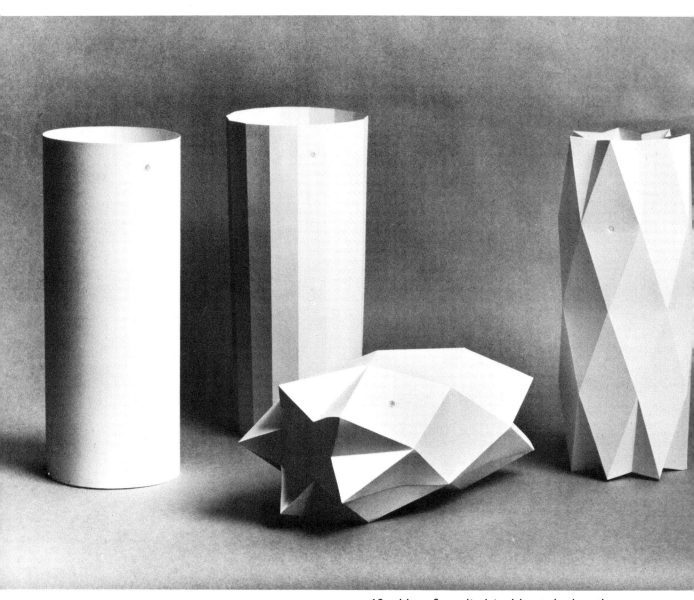

69   Ideas for cylindrical lampshades: the
pierced holes are fixed over wire supports

Lampshades

Good lighting creates a pleasant atmosphere in any home; it can be achieved easily by making a couple of new lampshades. These need not be expensive, so can be replaced at will. Cartridge paper makes excellent lampshades – the light shining through is pleasing, and there is no need to treat the paper with anything.

Some of the ways of shaping paper discussed previously may have already given the idea of making a lampshade. A cylindrical formation could be used quite successfully for a hanging light (figure 69). The simple, plain tube, the one with vertical scorings, or perhaps the more elaborate one with diagonal scored crossing lines could be used. Do not make the tube too narrow, as the electric bulb should be a fair distance from the paper, to prevent scorching, and to ensure an even distribution of light.

Method

When making the tube be careful to stick the overlapping edges neatly, with a quick drying adhesive (this join will later be kept away from view).

Make two holes opposite each other near the top rim, with the knitting needle. The lampshade will be hung in position by these two apertures, depending, of course,

70   *A more complex cylindrical lampshade*

upon the kind of flex used. With a *twisted flex* only one piece of wire, which is a bit longer than the diameter of the lampshade, is needed. Bend the wire slightly, in the middle, and bend the tips of the sloping down wires up. Push the wire through the twisted flex and hang the lampshade by pushing the upturned ends of the support through the two holes. The bulb should be positioned half-way down the tube. If the flex is *smooth* two wires of similar design must be placed each side of the flex and joined together and in position with *Sellotape* (*Scotch tape*). A concertina-type pleated lampshade can be hung in the same way, if it is not too large (figure 70).

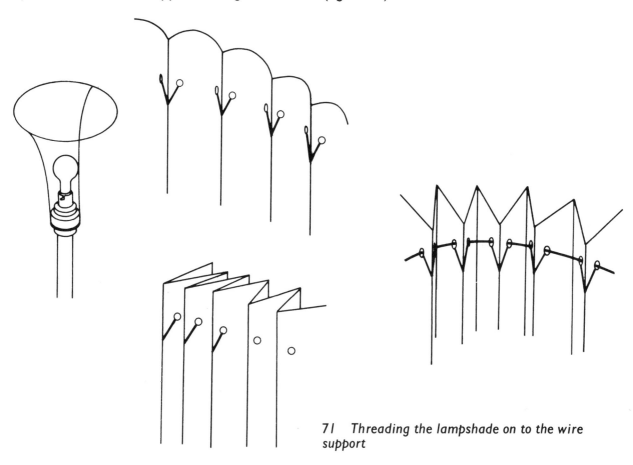

71 *Threading the lampshade on to the wire support*

Standing lamps

For a standing lamp a light fixture with a
ring is needed, and a pleated or fluted
lampshade is fixed to it as follows. Once
the paper has been pleated, pinch the first
fold firmly and make a hole, with the knitting
needle, near the top edge and the crease.
Bring the second pleat forward to the first,
and pierce through this layer, keeping the
needle in position. Repeat all the way round,
piercing the holes in the same place in every
pleat. Then make diagonal cuts with the
scissors, from the ridges up to the holes; join
the ends of the formation on the inside with
Sellotape (*Scotch tape*), so that the edges of the
paper just meet.

To thread the lampshade on to the wire
frame, loosen the pleating, place the frame
inside the lampshade and start slipping the
'V' cuts over the wire, so the holes rest on the
ring. In this way the frame will support the
whole lampshade, so that it hangs down
vertically.

To make the shade flare out at the lower
edge, another row of holes must be pierced
nearer the top, above the wire, and a ribbon
or soft cord threaded through to draw the
top part of the pleating together. The holes
can be made by piercing with the scissors,
and then poking a knitting needle through
to make them equal and even (figure 71).

A more elaborate formation with pushed
through parts, like the lampshade illustrated
in figure 73, will also help the shade to flare
outwards. Notice the pleating on this shade –
although the cuts are on the same level and
close together, they do not join (there are
narrow strips in the pleating to divide them).

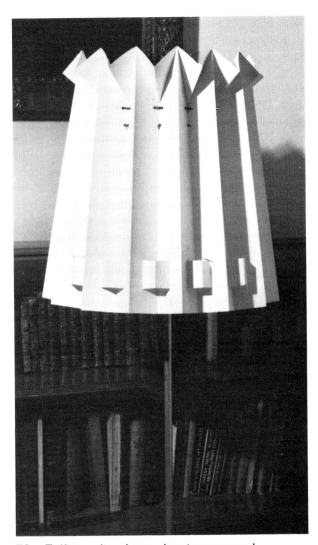

72 *Tall standing lamp showing reversed
pleating at the top edge of the shade and
protruding formations nearer the bottom*

73 Attractive table lamp, napkin holder covering an old jam jar, and two birds

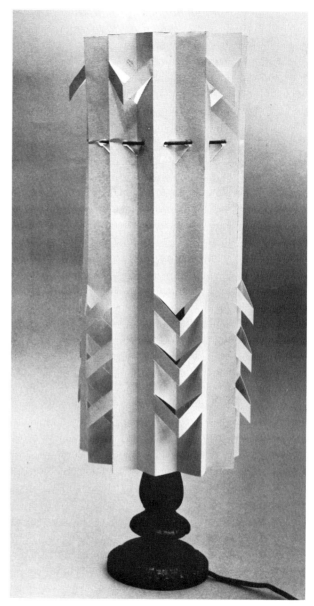

74 Table lamp with an attractive shade

Decorations

On special occasions – a children's party, birthday, anniversary – and particularly at Christmas time, it is pleasant to create a festive mood: imaginative paper sculpture decorations are easily made and attractive. The following ideas use inexpensive white paper (eg a pad of good writing paper), but the results will not look cheap.

Stars can be used in a variety of ways (see pages 29 to 35 for the method of making them).

Even a small Christmas tree takes up precious space in a modern home. Instead, take a couple of fir or evergreen branches and place them firmly in a jug or vase. They will give a very festive air if hung with a number of different stars and placed in a prominent position in the room.

Stars pinned on to a plain curtain make another attractive decoration. Attaching a short loop to the tip of the star will help it stay in position, even when the curtains are drawn back in the daytime.

A mobile of paper sculpture items is easy to make and very effective. The one shown in figure 76 uses stars. The cleanly cut surfaces reflect light, and the mobile will look particularly attractive if hung where there is some movement – in the hall or living room, or on the staircase – so that it spins round and sparkles.

Angels are characteristic of Christmas.

75 Stars make an attractive Christmas decoration

71

A 'choir' of them suspended from the ceiling, with the whiteness of the sculptures gleaming in the light, would look most effective. Instructions follow for making a 'basic angel', but all the different features can be varied.

Method

Sheets from a writing pad are ideal for this purpose: one sheet will make one angel. Following the pattern shown in figure 78, fold a sheet of paper in half and cut it into two with a sharp knife.

76 *A star mobile is interesting to watch*
How to make a mobile: Suspend one star at each end of a stick and find the balance of it by placing the stick at the approximate point on the blade of a pair of scissors. When the point of balance has been found, make a notch. Attach to this a length of thread, tying the other end to one of the next stick. At the other end of this stick, suspend a star. Find the balance of the second stick, make a notch and attach a thread – and a small mobile is created. When making a mobile, always start at the lowest level

77 *A 'choir' of angels is an appropriate Christmas decoration*

One of the halves makes the robe. Curl one corner inwards and the other one, along the shorter edge, outwards. These curled corners give the robe a sculptural appearance, and also indicate movement.

Fold the other half sheet in half again, and separate it into two parts. Following figure 78, fold one of these parts lengthwise and cut out a pair of wings as indicated. The top part of the curve will form the nose and eyebrows (see page 41), and a pair of hands can be cut from the remaining triangle at the base of the wings. Fringe the lower part of the wings to indicate feathers.

Place the wings at the centre of the narrow uncurled edge of the robe. Match the edge with the centre cut out piece, and glue or pin them into position (the point of the pin should be outside the angel and pointing downwards). Overlap the two top corners of the robe and fix them with a blob of glue.

Fold the remaining piece of paper in half and cut it apart, to use as indicated in figure 78. One piece will be the angel's head, adorned with curls. Cut out the oval shape of the face, the eyelids and the mouth; cut the strands of hair each side of the face, and along the top edge, curling them to make a hairstyle after the head has been shaped by sticking one side edge over the other to form a tube. Curve the nose part and fix it to the head at the back, making the nose and eyebrows cast a shadow on to the face. The face should now have the eyelids curved outwards and the mouth shaped.

Cut the final piece of paper lengthwise into two parts, and halve one of these parts lengthwise again. These latter two pieces will be used for cuffs. The other piece can either be a sheet of music, or it can be rolled into a recorder or a trumpet, which the angel will hold in his hands (which will be fixed to the cuffs).

Make a loop in a piece of thread and slip the knot under the protruding point of the pin between the wings, to hang the angel in position. The basic form is simple but all the details can be varied – facial expressions, hairstyles, ways of arranging the cuffs, etc.

78   Each angel (whether large or small) is made from one sheet of paper

overleaf
79   One angel is playing the flute, the others are singing

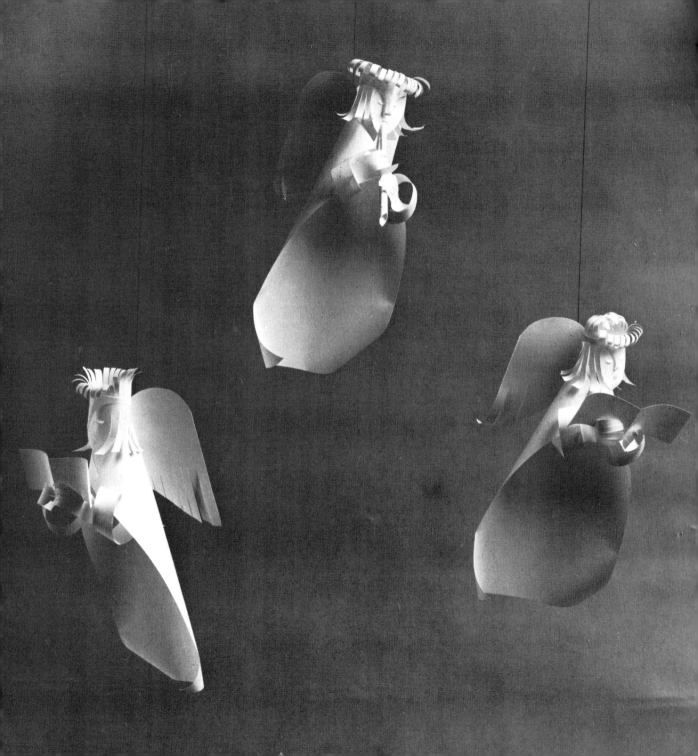

Birds Paper birds make another attractive decoration, either placed on bare branches or among green foliage. Again a pad of good writing paper will be useful to make a number of similar-sized birds.

A paper bird consists of two parts: the head and wings; and the body and tail. Take two sheets, cutting one lengthwise and the other across the width. The lengthwise strips will be used for the head and wings, and the other for the body parts.

Following figure 80, twist the lengthwise strip, at its middle, into a cone, with two equal ends. Fix the cone with glue, and after this has dried, pierce two small holes each side of the pointed part. This gives the bird's head with two eyes and a beak.

Then take one of the rectangular pieces and cut the narrower edges into strips. Turn one of the fringed ends over and make a crease: this fringe will be curved downwards with the scissors, and the other end's strips will be curled upwards. Then overlap the ends of the folded ridge (after a curling treatment) to form a cone. Fix this with glue, and slip this body part with its tail into the cone of the head, applying a blob of glue. The wings can be curved outwards at the tips, and the lower corner may also be cut away in a curved line.

To make the tails look longer and more exotic, only cut the strips at one end, and shape the other end into the cone to fit into the head part. Alternatively, take a much longer piece of paper.

To place the birds on branches, either slip a small branch into the inside of the body or, if it has foliage, slip a leaf into the body, and this will hold the bird in position. Short cuts at the edges of the body can also be used to wedge the bird against a branch, or into a leaf. The birds can be used as decorations,

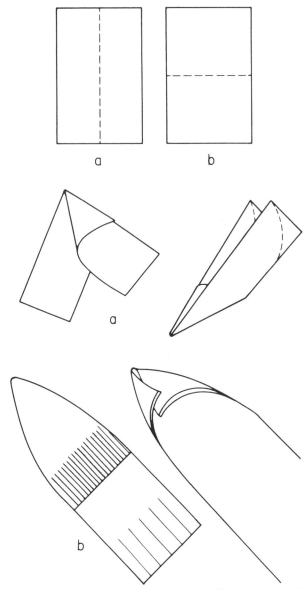

80 *Making the birds from halves of two pieces of paper*

like stars, placed on branches, or they can be part of a gay table decoration, making a children's party more festive.

Table decorations

Elaborate table decorations were common in the past. Some Renaissance cooks not only excelled themselves in their fantastic culinary achievements but also produced wonderful decorations of spun sugar and other confectionery for the princely or royal tables. Later, in the eighteenth century, the new craze for porcelain replaced these candy figures. Porcelain was fashioned into the most luxurious table decorations. Nowadays we do not live in such style but our surroundings and way of life can be more pleasant and gracious by using a little imagination.

Dinner by candlelight with a few friends can be so pleasant, particularly if candle and place-card holders have been made (figure 82) and the table has been laid and decorated in an attractive or unusual manner. Flowers are often expensive· so why not make paper ones to enhance the centre of your dinner table (figure 83).

A variation of the flowers illustrated in figures 45–48 is simple to make but very attractive. The stems are thin dowelling (drinking straws could be used) holding ordinary bottle corks into which holes are drilled. The corks support the flowers, which are made from good writing paper. This should be springy enough to lend itself to small and intricate forms. Measure the circumference of the cork with a strip of paper to ensure the right size pieces of paper are used for the flowers. Cut a few longish rectangles, the shorter side to go round the cork. Draw margins on each side of the sheet, score along the short edges, fold the

paper so that the short edges match, and cut in thin strips from the folded ridge to the marginal line, then bend the margins in the same direction only. Previously, with the star-flower formations, the margins were bent toward each other, to overlap – but not in this case. The stems can be painted or a strip of coloured paper glued spiral-wise will make them more attractive, but they can be left the natural colour of the wood.

Next fix the top margin (which is bent downwards) along the top edge of the cork, using quick drying adhesive. When this is dry apply some glue to the bottom edge of the cork, and fix the lower margin all the way round, covering the cork. The paper should just meet edge to edge. In this way the strips have formed a rather exotic flower shape. To cover where the stem joins the cork, take a strip of paper wide enough to to be cut lengthwise into fine strips along only one edge. Curl the fringe and fix it to the bottom of the flower by the plain edge, all the way round. A simple cone at the top may just put the finishing touch to the creation, emphasising the difference between the cones and the delicate filigree formations.

After making the first one, start thinking about the many variations which are possible. Two of the flowers shown in the table decoration (figure 83) have no cone centres; as a variation a longish piece of paper was used which was cut into a fine fringe at both narrow ends. After curling the ends, the piece was first glued round the cork, and then the filigree part was fixed round it. Of course two or even three of these formations can be used on one flower.

opposite
81 Birds on a branch are an amusing decoration

82 *A quick way to decorate the table for a special occasion: the candle is firmly fixed in a holder which is disguised by a paper sculpture creation*

opposite
83 *A more elaborate decoration*

Coloured paper sculpture

When using coloured paper, it is important to choose one with a matt surface, because of light and shadow effects. A shiny surface creates unwanted reflections which may destroy the whole appearance of the work unless, of course, this kind of effect is wanted.

The Father Christmas with reindeers sculpture (figures 84, 85) was made entirely

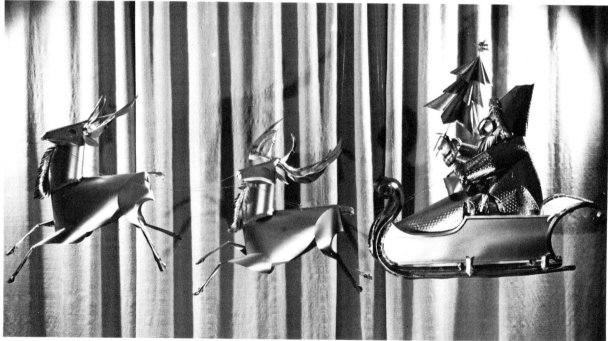

84   Father Christmas with reindeer, made from different textured gold foil-papers

opposite
Plate 5   The Aquarium   *see also figure 90*

85 *Father Christmas and reindeer have a thin batten reinforcement to hold the complex paper sculpture, so that it can be hung up*

of gold-foil card, using different textures to show the formations to advantage. Being an item 'in the round' it had to be reinforced inside with thin angular strips of wood (figure 86). Light constructions were placed inside the reindeers – along the body, with pieces attached along the neck, and one wire loop at the head, and another at the tail end, where nylon threads are fixed on. The sleigh was reinforced with similar batons (inside, at the bottom edges), for correct suspension. A cross bar was placed inside the shoulders of the figure, to connect with the sleigh at the bottom, and a thread was attached to it which comes out through his forehead but is disguised by the fur trimming on the hood.

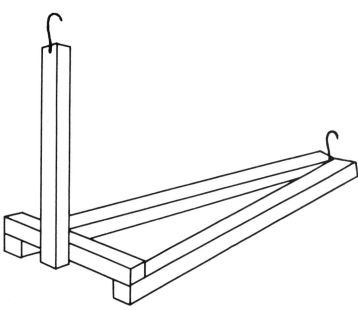

86 *Light batten construction with hooks, so the reindeer can be hung up*

opposite
87 Couple of 1830 *Free standing sculpture in coloured papers: one support stick for each figure*

above
88 St George and the Dragon *Very large panel made from coloured paper, with part exhibition poster used for caparison. 1968–9 Camden Arts Centre, London*

opposite
89 Queen Elizabeth I and Sir Walter Raleigh *Coloured paper sculpture built into a wooden box: easy to handle and keep when used for educational purposes*

84

90 The Aquarium *is made from coloured papers, some gold and silver foil papers. The support for the large fish is a stick concealed in the exotic plant. The paper-sculpture is in the Oxford City and County Museum's Education Department. See also plate 5*

opposite
91 You too can help *An appeal's display in coloured papers; the wording is made from strips of paper*

Paper sculpture lettering

First and foremost lettering ought to be legible, so it is usually treated in a two-dimensional way. Nevertheless the Roman alphabet started as three-dimensional incised symbols, readable because of the play of light and shadows within words composed of capital letters – so why not paper sculpture letters?

The basic idea behind those illustrated (figures 92–5) was to make each from one piece of paper, to create a three-dimensional effect – by cutting, bending, curling, scoring or folding – which was also legible. The reader is encouraged to make further experiments.

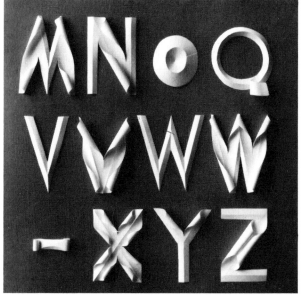

92

93

opposite 94

PAPER SCULPTURE

PAPER SCUPTURE

This book has introduced various approaches to the creative handling of paper in a three-dimensional way, from the simplest to the most complicated. It is always important to consider the play of light and shadows, the main factor when appreciating and enjoying any sculpture, irrespective of the material from which it is created.

The ingredient of surprise should never be discounted when making something, so it is now left to the reader to experiment, to discover new ways and perhaps to achieve unexpected results.

A brief outline of the historical background to paper sculpture

Paper sculpture was first created in the form of class-room exercises called 'Composition of Forms and Planes'. It was taught between 1911 and 1914 by Wojciech Jastrzębowski (1884–1963), within the subject of Applied Arts, at the private school of painting for young women run by Maria Niedzielska in Cracow, Poland. Professor Jastrzębowski's intention was to illustrate the problems of composition in an abstract way, using two-dimensional shapes, three-dimensional forms and related space. His ideas were based on the principle of designing by utilising contrast and rhythm, understanding the material being used, and by applying the right working processes and tools.

As paper was readily available in the studio, and was a good, cheap medium it was used to demonstrate the principles involved, especially questions of three-dimensional design. The interesting results encouraged Jastrzębowski to continue this activity at the Academy of Fine Arts in Warsaw, where he was invited to teach in 1923 and later to become its Rector.

Some of his pupils continued to use paper sculpture as a means of expressing themselves, for example Jan Kurzatkowski, who produced some striking items for display purposes in the early 1920s. Later on several talented graphics students took this new technique up, producing some interesting work for the Polish pavilions at the International Exhibitions in Paris in 1937, and New York in 1939. The names of Edward Manteuffel (1908–44) and Antoni Waywód (1908–44) are notable.

Tadeusz Lipski, who was also a graduate of the Warsaw Academy, popularised paper sculpture in England during the last war, and is now practising the art in New York; and artists in many countries have taken it up.

Suppliers

Papers of all kinds

Fred Aldous Limited
The Handicrafts Centre
37 Lever Street
Manchester M60 1UX

E J Arnold & Company Limited
(School Suppliers)
Butterley Street
Leeds LS10 1AX

Arts and Crafts
10 Byram Street
Huddersfield HD1 1DA

Crafts Unlimited
21 Macklin Street
London WC2

Dryad Limited
Northgates
Leicester

F G Kettle
127 High Holborn
London WC1

Nottingham Handcrafts Company
(School Suppliers)
Melton Road
West Bridgeford
Nottingham

Paperchase Products Limited
216 Tottenham Court Road
London W1

George Rowney and Company Limited
10 Percy Street
London W1

Winsor and Newton Limited
Wealdstone
Harrow
Middlesex (and branches)

Reeves and Sons Limited
Lincoln Road
Enfield
Middlesex (and branches)

Papers are also obtainable from most stationers and artists colourmen in Britain and the USA, from whom also Stanley knives (craft knives) and adhesives can be bought.

WITHDRAWN
No longer the property of the
Boston Public Library.
Sale of this material benefits the Library